Executive Director Succession Plan and Search Process

Toolkit #4

Strategies for developing your ED succession plan and ED search

Marilyn L. Donnellan, MS

Ron Soto, MSW, MPH

Executive Director Succession Plans and Search Process

Nonprofit Toolkits
Available at
www.amazon.com/author/mldonnellan

Tool #1: Volunteer Handbooks
Tool #2: The Top Twenty Sustainability Strategies for Nonprofits
Tool #3: Becoming a Tech-Focused Nonprofit
Tool#4: ED Succession Plans & Search Process

Published by CreateSpace
©2018, by Marilyn L. Donnellan, Author

All rights reserved. This includes the right to reproduce any portion of this book in any form. The author and publisher specifically disclaim any responsibility for any liability, loss, or risk, personal or otherwise, incurred consequently, directly or indirectly, of the use and application of any of the contents of this book. Although every precaution has been taken in the preparation of this book, the publisher and authors assume no responsibility for errors or omissions.

ISBN-10-1720307261
ISBN-13-978-1720307266 CreateSpace

Table of Contents	Page
Introduction	4
Part I: ED Succession Plans	**6**
Chapter One: Challenges	6
Chapter Two: Roles & Responsibilities	9
Chapter Three: Emergency Succession Plans	12
Chapter Four: The Succession Plan	19
Part II: The ED Search Process	**21**
Chapter One: Challenges	21
Chapter Two: Essential Steps Before Beginning the Search Process	24
Chapter Three: Forming the Search Committee	33
Chapter Four: The Work of the Committee	38
Chapter Five: Orientation of the ED	44
Chapter Six: Evaluation of the Search Process	47
Figures	**Page**
#1: The Top Twenty Sustainability Strategies	5
#2: Governance Structures	25
#3: Core Elements Chart & Rating Scale	28
#4: Board & Staff Roles & Responsibilities	30
Addendums	**Page**
A: ED Job Description	49
B: ED Core Competencies	52
C: ED Succession Planning Committee Job Description	57
D: Boards of Directors Job Descriptions	60
E. ED Search Committee Job Description	64
F: ED Resume Rating Scale	66
About the Authors	**68**

All material, figures and addendums are copyrighted and based on the books in the Nonprofit Management Simplified series, ©2017, CharityChannel Press, by M. L. Donnellan, MS

Introduction

Executive director (ED) succession planning and the ED search process are two of the most important responsibilities of the board of directors of any nonprofit. But few know how to go about developing policies and procedures for these issues. This guide will provide you with step-by-step strategies adaptable to any nonprofit.

Developing an executive director succession plan is strategy #9 in *The Top Twenty Nonprofit Sustainability Strategies, Toolkit #2 (Fig. 1)*.

But a succession plan must also be complemented by a companion ED search process. Too often executive director search committees scramble to hunt for the next executive director with little thought to the profound impact their efforts will have on the future of their nonprofit. In their rush to fill the position, they fail to consider what type of ED they need, based on what phase of organizational development their nonprofit is in, and what leadership they need for long-term sustainability.

Or, because they do not understand the duties of the ED, the committee will focus on hiring someone whose work experience and skills fit with the mission of the nonprofit rather than on the critical core management competencies they need.

Well written ED succession plans will ensure the long-term sustainability of the vision and mission of your nonprofit, helping you avoid the pitfalls of not planning for the day your ED will leave. And, a written search plan will help your nonprofit select the right ED to fit your needs.

This toolkit will help you do both. The toolkit provides an in depth and practical look at every aspect of these two critical board responsibilities.

Fig. 1: The Top Twenty Sustainability Strategies

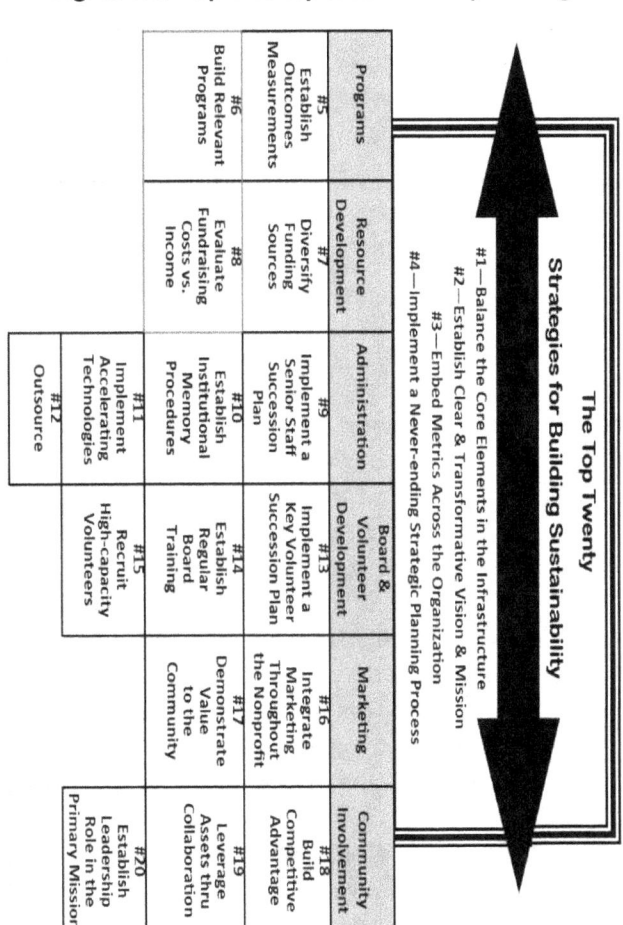

Part I – Executive Director Succession Plans

Chapter One: Challenges

Effective succession planning increases the likelihood that a nonprofit will have the strong leadership required to increase its organization's service capacity, program effectiveness, and long-term stability and sustainability.

Lack of formal plans

A recent study of succession planning in nonprofits organizations, including a sample of 250 agencies by the Center for Nonprofit Strategy and Management, found 69 percent of the boards surveyed do not have a succession plan in place for the current executive director or CEO. Seventy-eight percent could not immediately name a successor if the current executive director or CEO were to leave the organization tomorrow. On average, nonprofit directors estimate that it would take 90 days to find a permanent replacement.

Does this sound like your organization? If so, you need an ED succession plan. Planning for leadership transition represents a proactive and responsible board of directors' action. It is just a matter of time before a leadership change will occur, whether due to an unexpected event, career advancement opportunity, or the anticipated transition of a long-term ED.

An ED succession plan can help your organization better face the funding and operational challenges often associated with the leadership void attributed to the transitions of executive directors.

Emergencies thwart planning

To prepare for the unexpected departure, as well as the planned departure of your ED, your succession plan should include two scenarios:

1. *Emergency Succession Planning*

This is a contingency plan process in place in the event the executive suddenly departs – either permanently or for an extended period, usually longer then the time it would take to fill the position. This plan should assure the continuous coverage of executive duties of the organization to fulfill funder contractual service, donor, and community activity commitments.

2. *Formal Succession Planning*

A formal process and steps would cover the future planned retirement (at least six months' notice), or the permanent departure of the ED.

Planning in isolation

An effective succession-planning process should not be developed in isolation by a board committee. Although it can be a challenge, a collaborative succession planning process is ideal. The board should include active participation of the incumbent executive, as well as key senior management staff.

Benefits

There are several benefits of this collaborative approach, including:

- *Solid foundation for operations*
  It will help create a collaborative, solid foundation for nonprofit operations, when transition occurs. Working as a team during this period of change will give a positive message to funders and stakeholders that the process of transition will happen smoothly.
- *Reduce staff concerns*
  It will reduce staff concerns because the transition process is transparent, and they can follow its planning and implementation. Whether the ED is replaced from within or from outside, the formal process, steps and selection process will be known.
- *Board members understand their roles*
  Board members will be clear about their roles and responsibilities contributing to a successful ED transition process. Since the current board members may not have all been members of the board when the succession plan was written and adopted, it can be very instructive and assuring for them to know ahead of time what the plan is.

Chapter Two: Roles & Responsibilities

There are specific roles and responsibilities of the various collaborative partners in developing the succession plan. Each partner must understand those roles and be trained on how to implement their responsibilities.

Board Members
- If board members know and understand the external and internal complexity and responsibilities of the executive director, they will be better able to assure comprehensive succession and search plans.
- Active board-level committees and the annual evaluation of the ED should ensure a knowledgeable board, especially if these are based on a board-approved core competencies document (Addendums A & B).
- Board members active in the external affairs of the nonprofit will continue to help leverage nonprofit funding, stakeholders and board contacts and expertise, especially during periods of leadership transition.
- A special committee or task force appointed by the board (Addendum C) should play a lead role in working with the executive and key management staff in the develop of succession plans that incorporate the various nonprofit funders, stakeholder groups and identify possible challenges and scenarios which could arise.
- The full board should review and approve the final succession plan and formulate and designate a board

committee to address transitional issues in the unexpected departure of the executive.
- The board-approved policy and plan should be incorporated into the Board Policy Manual (see *Nonprofit Management Simplified: Board & Volunteer Development and Nonprofit Toolkit #1: Volunteer Handbooks)*

Executive Director
- The ED must maintain open communication with the board chair regarding their job satisfaction, future, possible departures under certain conditions, or available opportunities. Often EDs or Board members (or both), hesitate to bring up ED departure issues or plans, because they think they would be encouraging it.
- Work with the board Succession Plan Committee to execute the planning process with other key staff involved.
- Implement staff development programs that promote a nonprofit culture of training, personal growth, and on-going professional development.
- Share key nonprofit liaison and operational duties with senior staff (as feasible), to assure good communication in the event of the ED's departure.
- Implement and communicate the succession plan with affected staff.
- Assist the board in reviewing the ED core competencies document on which the ED job description and performance review are based (Addendum A and B)

Key Senior Staff
- Actively support and provide input into planning areas they oversee or implement.
- Continue to provide quality administrative, funding, stakeholder relations/communication, and services to clients in the absence of the ED and during any transition.
- Support the implementation of the successful transition of the new executive and provide program and organizational information as requested.

Chapter Three: Emergency Succession Plan

The purpose of an emergency succession plan as defined previously is to ensure continuous coverage of executive duties, critical to the ongoing operations and organization's sustainability, in the event of an emergency departure of the executive.

The pre-planning for this plausible scenario with ED and key staff input before it occurs, will contribute to a more effective plan to ensure some normalcy in external relationships and operational effectiveness, during this potentially stressful period.

The emergency plan addresses issues related to both permanent (executive will not return) and temporary (executive will return after unplanned absence such as illness, etc.) replacement. At a minimum, the following planning steps should be addressed in your Emergency Plan:

Step 1: Executive Committee Convenes

The board chair is empowered by a board approved policy to inform the executive committee of the unplanned departure of the executive and related issues (departure date, circumstances, immediate contact information, etc.). The succession plan policy should authorize the board chair to meet with the executive committee to confirm the procedures outlined in the emergency succession plan and/or to make any modifications the executive committee deems appropriate, and then to implement the terms of the plan.

Step 2: Formulate board of directors' policy to authorize the executive committee to be convened by the board chair and to implement the ED emergency succession plan.

Step 3: Identify the key spokesperson or contact for the organization until the new executive is temporarily replaced or permanently hired.

Step 4: Formulate and define internal communication plan to include a departure date (if applicable), transition plan, replacement issues, temporary appointments, etc. Include procedures for updating staff, board, committee members and volunteers. Be sure to keep people informed of progress in replacing ED.

Step 5: Define external communication plan. Include targeted key stakeholder groups, individuals, funders/donors. Name an interim spokesperson, contacts, etc., to keep stakeholders informed on progress toward filling the ED position.

Step 6: Define interim executive key responsibilities. This plan should ensure the essential, continuous coverage of executive duties of the organization to fulfill funder service goals, donor, and community activity commitments. A more detailed updating and matching of nonprofit skill and abilities needed will be included in the ED search process, as outlined in Part II.

In small nonprofits, it might be a board member stepping in and taking on the ED responsibilities. Or, in a larger nonprofit, an existing senior staff manager, or a retired executive hired from the outside might be hired until the ED returns, if the vacancy is temporary. Other tasks include:

a. Update the ED job description to ensure the interim executive responsibilities and hiring requirements promote the organization's sustainability. List key core competencies (Addendum B), expertise, experience and required leadership style. Does the organization need someone who is a highly controlling leader or one who exhibits a more participatory style of management?

b. Attach current executive job description (Addendum A). Position description should be updated as needed, preferably during the organization's annual strategic planning sessions.

Step 7: Outline authority and restrictions for interim executive.

- In what areas does the interim ED have full authority to make decisions?
- What areas do they have where they must seek prior approval from the board chair or executive committee?
- Are they allowed to make commitments for the organization? If so, in what areas?
- What authority do they have for financial expenditures? Are there any constraints?
- What area of the organization are they to focus their attention on? (Fig. 3)

Examples of key activities to include in this step might be:

- Serve with integrity and strength as the organization's primary leader, representative and spokesperson to the community
- Support the board of directors, including preparing executive reports and attending board committee meetings
- Lead the staff management team
- Participate in the recruitment and selection for directly supervised staff

    Note: Be cautious in this recruitment activity, especially if the emergency succession plan is being implemented because the ED suddenly terminated employment and you will be hiring a new ED. That's because the new ED should be the one to hire their own new staff. Only in an emergency should the interim do the hiring.

- Manage initiatives related to building organizational capacity, sustainability and the strategic plan
- Establish, maintain and cultivate relations with donors, foundations and other stakeholders and volunteers
- Execute resource development plans and fund-raising strategies.

    Clearly outline authority and restrictions of the appointed interim ED. For example: *The interim ED shall have the full authority for decision making and independent action, except for the following which must be approved by the board:*
    1. *All financial expenditures over $10,000*
    2. *Termination of staff*
    3. *Issues which may negatively impact the organization's reputation in the community.*

Step 8: Determine compensation for the interim executive. This decision will depend on the financial state of the nonprofit. Compensation policies and salary ranges for an interim might include the following considerations:
- A board member appointment might be with a stipend payment, or a salaried position, plus reimbursement for costs incurred
- Existing ED current salary, plus a percentage for an interim EDS hired from outside the organization
- If a current staff person, the interim ED shall receive a temporary salary increase to the entry level salary range of the ED position, or up to a specific percentage above their current salary, whichever is greater.

Step 8. Establish process to appoint interim executive. The executive committee should outline procedures for:
- Considering and interviewing internal senior staff for the interim position
- Appointing a board member to fill the position
- Hiring a temporary person from outside the nonprofit.

Outlining the steps in the process in advance will allow for a timelier and less stressful process of making an interim appointment. Ideally, in nonprofits with a formal management structure, the emergency plan should include cross-training of management-level staff in case of a need for an interim appointment. For example, such a process and policy might be stated this way:

In preparation for the eventual departure of the ED, the ED shall develop and executive a plan for leadership and management training in the core operational areas

(Fig. 3). Should the interim assignment be longer than three months, or if extenuating circumstances exist, a secondary backup for the interim ED will be identified.

Notice that the focus with this type of plan and process is still on the fulfillment of the interim responsibilities. The executive committee might also consider the option of splitting executive duties among the designated appointees from within the current management staff.

Note: Another caution, here: This may seem like a simple solution but, depending on the length of the ED absence, it can create undue pressure on existing staff and result in dissatisfaction and frustration, especially if there is not additional compensation given to the fill-in staff.

Step 10: Determine board oversight and support of interim ED. The board's executive committee will have the responsibility of monitoring and supporting the work of the interim staff or ED. Regular meetings should be established with designated board representatives and the interim ED to discuss key issues and any support requested by the acting ED. Include in your plan when and where such meetings will occur.

Step 11: Develop process to select permanent new ED. If the nonprofit has not already prepared for an internal successor for the eventual departure of the ED, the board chair should appoint the committee and execute the search process, as outlined in Part II of this guide. The search committee will be responsible for conducting the search (or selecting an outside hiring firm), interviewing candidates and finalists, and recommending a final candidate to the board for approval.

Step 12: Approve the emergency succession plan. The written succession plan should be approved by the executive committee and then presented to the board for review, final approval and signatures. Be sure the approved policy includes the date approved by the board. Copies of the emergency succession plan should be disbursed to:
- The organization's policies and procedures manual
- Board president
- Current executive director
- Human Resources department
- Corporate attorney

When implemented, copies of the plan will also be given to:
- Interim ED, or
- Temporary staff appointees to the position
- Any back-up appointees.

These twelve steps will help you to develop an emergency succession plan and process to implement when there is an unexpected departure of the ED. However, development of a formal succession plan, long before the ED submits their resignation, is also necessary.

©2017, Nonprofit Management Simplified, CharityChannel Press

Chapter Four: The Succession Plan

The formal succession planning is a process that is in place for a future planned retirement or permanent exit of the executive. But there are some important issues to consider before putting the plan together.

Issues to consider

1. Current ED wants to provide input

While it might be important for the departing ED to support the succession-planning process, they must be able to deal with personal issues related to it and not interfere. The board must determine how much input is acceptable.

2. Long time ED

The transition can be more challenging when an organization founder or long-standing ED is planning to depart. The focus on planning should be on the organizational leadership and administrative needs and not on selecting a predecessor who necessarily resembles the departing ED. The organization may be at a different phase of development or require a new strategic direction which requires a different set of abilities and skills than when the departing ED was hired.

3. Program skills vs. management skills

While your nonprofit's mission is your driving focus, you should not hire a new ED who is simply an advocate of your mission and has strong program delivery skills but who lacks the management skill sets in all the core elements (Fig. 3) required to move your nonprofit forward.

Essential questions you need to discuss as part of the succession planning process, are very similar to the questions you will need to ask yourself to prepare for a planned ED search process.

Part II: The Search Process

Chapter One: Challenges

Before we get into the specifics of setting up the ED search process, let's look at some of the typical problems and challenges associated with the process. I've either run into these myself during the hiring process, or I've seen them as a consultant for nonprofits who are trying to hire an ED.

1. *Rushing the process*
Because few nonprofits have implemented a succession plan (Part I), when the ED suddenly departs or tells the board they are resigning, there is often a frantic, last-minute effort to hire a warm body, without making sure they are a good fit.

2. *Untrained search committee*
Often search committees have not been trained in how to do their job. The board looks for anyone interested in serving on the committee, rather than looking for individuals with qualifications and experience in personnel hiring and management.

3. *No exit interview of ED*
Scrambling to fill the position, the search committee usually fails to interview the outgoing ED to find out why they are leaving or what they liked or didn't like about the job. This means the committee is flying blind on some very important issues.

4. *No policies and procedures for succession planning or search process*

Because there are no written policies and procedures for the hiring process, the search committee is forced to figure it out as they go and hope they get it right.

5. *No clue what type of ED is needed*

Does the nonprofit need a change agent or a maintainer to continue the status quo? Often the search committee isn't sure what the ED's job is, either, so it makes for a case of the blind leading the blind in the hiring process. This challenge is exacerbated if neither the board nor the search committee understands the current governance structure of the nonprofit.

6. *Don't know if they should use a professional search firm*

First, they don't know what a search firm can do, but secondly, they don't know what it would cost or if they could afford it.

7. *No understanding of the role of the board versus the role of the ED*

Without understanding governance structure or the roles of the board and ED, the search committee cannot possibly match the right ED to the needs of the nonprofit.

8. *No process infrastructure*

Without a written process, budget or timeline, the search committee will be forced to flounder around, trying to figure it out as they go, wasting valuable time and money.

©2017, Nonprofit Management Simplified, CharityChannel Press

9. No follow-up or orientation strategies for new ED
Once the search committee has recommended an ED to the board, they think their work is done. Consequently, no one thinks to do an orientation with the new ED, leaving them to figure it out on their own while struggling to get to know the people, the community, the policies and procedures, as well as the programs of the organization.

Chapter Two: Essential Steps Before Beginning Search Process

Before the search committee can even begin its work, there are several issues to be addressed, both organizationally and related to the ED. These can best be addressed by a task force appointed by the board, or by a couple of board members who will ultimately be on the search committee.

Organizational Issue: Governance

I mentioned governance structure in the fifth challenge in the last chapter. Why is this important for the search committee to know? Every nonprofit is operating under a specific type of legal governance structure. If an ED is hired who has never worked in your nonprofit's type of governance (Fig. 2), it can create problems.

Let's suppose the new ED is used to working with a lot of volunteer, board-level committees (administrative or management style of governance). But your nonprofit has very few committees because you are more of a policy governing board. If neither the search committee or the board takes this issue into consideration, the new ED could be in over their head and not know how to function under your type of board and governance structure.

As you can see in Fig. 2, the various governance structures of nonprofits profoundly impact the duties of the ED and the board. If the search committee fails to take this into consideration, it could be a huge problem for both.

Fig. 2: Governance Structures

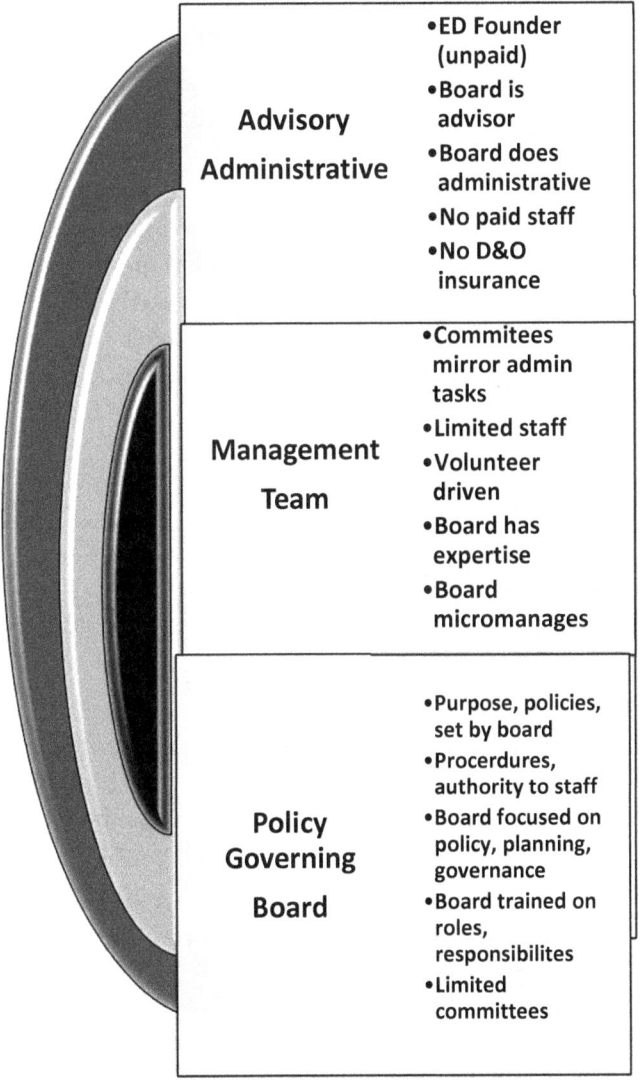

Advisory Administrative	• ED Founder (unpaid) • Board is advisor • Board does administrative • No paid staff • No D&O insurance
Management Team	• Commitees mirror admin tasks • Limited staff • Volunteer driven • Board has expertise • Board micromanages
Policy Governing Board	• Purpose, policies, set by board • Procerdures, authority to staff • Board focused on policy, planning, governance • Board trained on roles, responsibilites • Limited committees

©2017, Nonprofit Management Simplified, CharityChannel Press

There are very big differences in ED styles and how they fit with the different board governance structures. Advisory and administrative governance structures are primarily volunteer-driven and rarely have paid staff. If there is an ED, they serve more as a secretary than a CEO. These are often very small nonprofits. The founder often runs the show and may resent any staff. The board will have a hard time letting go of the administrative tasks they have been doing. If this type of nonprofit is transitioning to a management team style of governance, it will require a strong ED to deal with a recalcitrant board.

The management team board is a hybrid of the administrative and governing board. The board wants to transition to a policy-setting, governing board but may have problems letting go. This may require an ED with a high level of negotiating and diplomacy skills, as well as someone who works well with the multiple volunteer committees. These are often mid-sized nonprofits (around $3 million annual budget).

The policy governing board will focus on policy setting and strategic planning, so the board members will be less involved and there will be very limited committees. These are generally larger nonprofits with a lot of staff. They are often called "institutional boards," as well because they are usually hospitals, large universities, etc. This type of nonprofit needs an ED with a lot of management skills for working with large numbers of staff.

Be sure the board member job description reflects the current governance structure (Addendum D)

Organizational Issue: Assessments

Before hiring an ED, the search committee needs to review any assessments available to determine the type of ED needed to address the weak areas. The Core Elements Assessment in the book, *Nonprofit Management Simplified: Board and Volunteer Development*, is a great tool the board and staff can use to get a comprehensive overview of every aspect of the organization.

Any areas showing 50% or less responses are an indication these need work and would require an ED with skills in those areas. This assessment is extremely helpful for jumpstarting a strategic planning process, too.

A simple rating tool is included in Fig. 3. Board and staff simply score the nonprofit on a scale of one to five in each of the areas shown. When the results are compiled, it will give the search committee an idea of where the perceived weak areas are in the nonprofit, thus inferring the skills needed by an incoming ED.

Organizational Issue: Strategic Plan

Does your nonprofit have a strategic plan which drives the staff and volunteer workplans, or does it sit on the shelf? When was it last updated? What role does the board play in its development? What role does the ED play in strategic planning? If you hire an ED with no experience developing strategic plans, it could be a problem.

A simplified strategic planning process is included in the book, *Nonprofit Management Simplified: Board and Volunteer Development*.

Fig. 3 – Core Elements Chart & Rating Scale

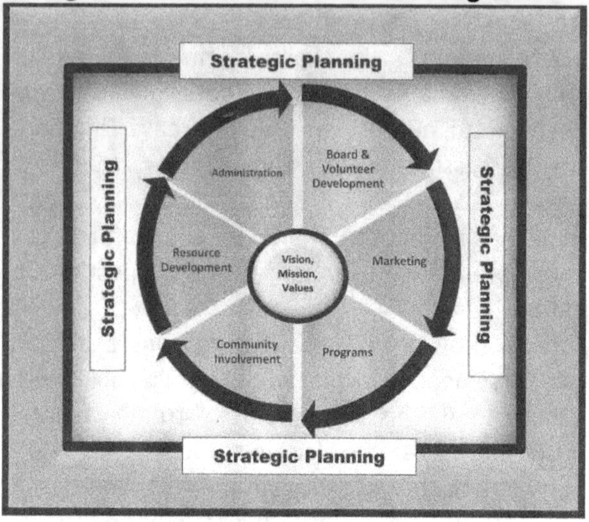

Diagram: A circular chart with "Vision, Mission, Values" at the center, surrounded by six core elements — Administration, Board & Volunteer Development, Marketing, Programs, Community Involvement, and Resource Development — all framed by "Strategic Planning" on all four sides.

Element	Rating
Board & Volunteer Dev.	
Marketing	
Programs	
Community Involvement	
Resource Development	
Administration	
Strategic Planning	

"5" = Excellent

Organizational Issue: Policies and Procedures

Does the nonprofit have a policies and procedures manual that clearly delineates between the two, and includes the dates when policies were approved? Is it computerized and hyperlinked so it can be easily updated? If there is no such manual, will it be the job of the new ED to develop one? How will you evaluate the potential candidates on their ability to develop such a critical manual? Far too many nonprofits do not have strong internal controls and then wonder why they get into trouble when they cannot locate important policies the board has already approved or needs to approve.

Role of the Board

Do board and staff understand the differences between their roles, responsibilities and lines of authority? Too few boards and staff are trained in this critical issue. If the new ED doesn't understand this, how can they be expected to train board and staff on the issue? Fig. 4 is a chart showing the critical relationships between board and staff.

A small nonprofit hired their first ED. The board was composed of parents of severely disabled adult-children who were working in the sheltered workshop they started. Because neither the board nor ED understood their roles and responsibilities, the board members were in the office every day trying to tell the ED how to do her job. Within six weeks, the new ED had a nervous breakdown and left the job.

This is an extreme, but true example of what can happen when there is a disconnect between roles and responsibilities of the board and ED.

Now that you have evaluated critical organizational and board issues, and completed some assessments, the search committee is better prepared to determine what type of ED your nonprofit needs.

Fig.4: Board & Staff Roles

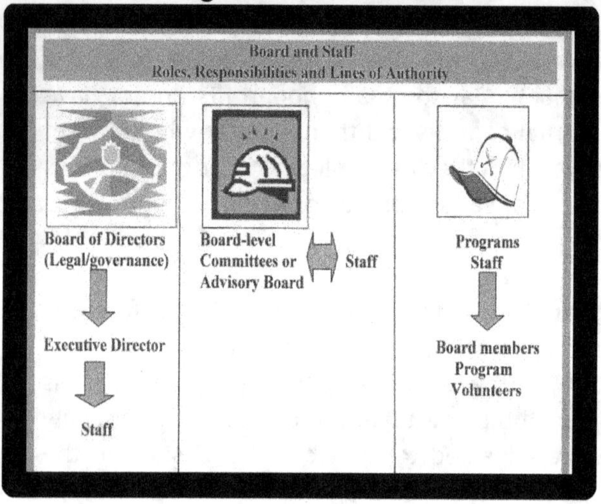

Board and Staff
Roles, Responsibilities and Lines of Authority

- Board of Directors (Legal/governance) → Executive Director → Staff
- Board-level Committees or Advisory Board ⇔ Staff
- Programs Staff → Board members, Program Volunteers

A change agent will help the nonprofit make essential transitions to new governance structures or expansions. A maintainer will keep a well-run organization running smoothly and build sustainability. Do you know which type you need? Do you need someone with a solid financial management and administrative background, a generalist (someone with a working knowledge of all the six core elements in Fig. 3), or an ED with a great resource development background?

©2017, Nonprofit Management Simplified, CharityChannel Press

Hiring an Interim ED

Given all the assessments and questions you answered, you should be better able to decide if you need an interim ED while the search committee is looking for the new ED. There are some specific things to consider:

1. Does the nonprofit need extra time to do a more thorough search? If so, maybe an interim ED is needed.
2. Is the organization going through some type of turmoil? The right interim ED (a retired ED or experienced consultant) can help stabilize the organization during a search process.
3. Does the search committee need an objective, unbiased internal operations or organizational assessment? An interim ED might be able to provide the kind of neutral analysis essential for the committee to prioritize the skills needed from the new ED.
4. Are there staff applying for the ED position? An interim ED makes sense if someone on staff might ordinarily serve as the interim, but they are applying for the ED position.
5. Are you limited in the number of staff who are qualified to be an interim ED because of your small size? If so, hiring an outsider might be a good idea.
6. Is there a need for someone neutral to come in and clean house, do staff performance evaluations, or to handle a difficult financial situation? They can sometimes make needed changes before the ED arrives. Just be sure you give them the authority to hire, fire and sign contracts, etc.

I strongly recommend an interim ED if there will be a gap of more than a week between when the current ED leaves and the new ED is hired. Even a part-time ED is better than none. Sometimes a retired ED can do the job. Interims are a great way to deal with negative issues, since they are objective. But pay them something; it's a tough job and needs to include compensation. Do not expect anyone to donate their time as an interim ED.

Chapter Three: Forming the Search Committee

The assessments are completed and now you have a much better idea of the type of ED you need. The task force or individuals assigned to gather all the information in chapter two are now ready to give the information to a duly-elected search committee.

Generally, search committees are appointed by the executive committee after first selecting a chair for the committee. The chair should be someone who fits the following criteria:

- A good communicator
- Understands the scope of the task
- A consensus builder
- Has the time and dedication
- Great leadership skills
- Can keep the committee focused
- Able to develop a job description

Addendum E includes examples of job descriptions for the chair and the search committee. Rewrite these to fit the criteria you are looking for and the duties you expect of them. These examples show them reporting to the board chair, with the executive committee doing the interviews of the three finalists selected by the committee, but that's up to you.

Some guidelines for the search committee members, include:

- Do not include staff since they will have a set of biases you don't need

- Do not include the former ED or founder for the same reason
- Do Include board members
- Limit the committee to no more than seven
- Include people with hiring experience, stakeholders, donors, good judges of people, good communicators, consensus builder
- Make sure whomever you recruit will have the time to commit to do this.

Budget Issues

Don't wait until you are in the middle of the search process to figure out where you are going to get the money to pay for the costs of the search process. In fact, the chair could begin putting a budget together before the committee is formed.

Some nonprofits think they are going to save money by not having an ED for a few months, while they are conducting the search process. Don't fall into that trap. Someone is going to have to fulfill those duties. If you don't have an interim ED, or a senior staff person who can temporarily assume the duties, and you wait until you hire the ED to fulfill those duties, things are going to be in a huge mess. It could take months or years to get things back into shape.

As you build the budget, add salary and benefits for the new ED. Don't think you can get away with paying less salary because the new ED might be a minority or a woman; that could come back to haunt you in an unfair hiring lawsuit.

Add into your budget costs, travel, hotel and meal costs for three to five finalists, or more. There might be special training costs for a new ED, especially if they are skilled in something you need, but not in another area specific to your mission. For example, a United Way, which specializes in workplace fundraising campaigns, may decide to hire someone who is good in administration, but they have no workplace campaign experience. But that is a trainable skill so the cost for the training needs to be built into the budget.

Train Committee Members

Few ED search committee members understand the ED job responsibilities, or the core competencies mentioned in Part I. So, how can they possibly understand who they should hire as an ED?

In some cases, search committee members are composed of people who have never done any hiring themselves. Without training, they might ask illegal questions which could put the nonprofit in legal jeopardy. That same ignorance might hinder their ability to look at resumes or rate them.

Without the right training in interview techniques or how to check references, committee members could make big mistakes.

The training should also include all the information already gathered from the assessments on the state of the nonprofit, as outlined in the first two chapters of this section. Committee members should have a strong since of urgency and be able to agree on a timeline. They need to take their jobs very seriously, since the ED they recommend could have a profound impact on the nonprofit and the community in the years to come.

Legal Issues

It is important the committee members understand critical legal issues before beginning the search process. If you have members with labor law training, so much the better; you are less likely to have the wrong questions asked during the interview process which could cause lawsuits:

- How old are you?
- Are you pregnant, or do you intend to get pregnant?
- When did you graduate from high school?
- Are you a homosexual, gay, lesbian or transgender?
- Are you disabled?

In the same category are benefits issues. The committee needs to know what benefits are available to the ED.

An experienced ED took a job where the employer insisted they had their own pension plan, for which he would be immediately qualified (vested) due to his previous years of experience. They even put it in writing. So, he took the job.

But, a nagging unease caused him to check with a benefits attorney to make sure what they promised him met federal ARISA legal requirements. After two years of investigation, it turned out the plan did not; what they promised him was illegal. Incensed at the deceit, the ED immediately resigned and filed a lawsuit against the nonprofit.

Advertising for the Position

Assuming you are not using a professional search firm, and you have finalized all the essential preparations, the committee is ready to advertise for the open position. Be

---

©2017, Nonprofit Management Simplified, CharityChannel Press

careful what you include in the position description. Do not include any descriptions which could be construed as illegal hiring questions: ethnicity requirements, age or sexual orientation. Keep the ad concise. Sometimes it is better to leave out the name of the nonprofit in the advertisement. For example, the ad might read:

Local nonprofit seeking executive director. Position requires the following experience and skills (list). Competitive salary and benefits. Submit resumes by (deadline) to (address or email).

Possible places to advertise include:
- Local media
- Trade journals
- LinkedIn
- www.indeed.com/non/profit
- www.careerbuilder.com/jobs-nonprofit
- www.bridgespan.org
- www.workforgood.org
- Associations of nonprofits

Have the resumes sent to a post office box or emailed to a committee member, not to the staff at the nonprofit. Determine which of the committee members will do the initial review of the resumes after putting together a rating scale based on your ED core competencies document. A simple rating form for resumes might look like Addendum F.

Allow at least a month for the first round of resumes to be sent in. Based on the totals on the rating form, narrow the possible candidates down to ten or twelve for the search committee to review and reduce it to the final three or four. Keep all the resumes you receive for at least year, just in case you need to take a second look.

©2017, Nonprofit Management Simplified, CharityChannel Press

Chapter Four: The Work of the Committee

The committee chair has been selected, a budget developed, organizational assessments are completed and the membership for the committee is finalized. You have even advertised for the position. But back up a minute, before they get started, the committee needs to have one critical discussion:

Should a professional search firm be hired?

There are advantages to hiring a firm who specializes in hiring executives, especially if you are a larger nonprofit (budget of $10 million or more). There are several things to consider:

- The local talent may be tapped out so there is a lack of qualified professionals in the area.
- Looking across multiple geographical areas takes a high level of knowledge and effort.
- An ED from outside your geographical area will have a much steeper learning curve than someone from within your community. But, the other side of the coin is they are often more objective and bring fresh perspectives to the job.
- Can reduce the time commitment needed by the volunteers.
- Increases objectivity.
- Identifies and screens initial finalists so the committee only interviews final few.
- Has the expertise to guide committee through finalist interviews and to check references of candidates.

- Be sure and check references of several search firms before hiring one.
- Request proposals and compare costs. They usually charge 25% to 33% of the estimated total annual ED compensation.
- Be sure to clarify roles of the search firm and the search committee.
- Require the firm to establish strong communication strategies with the search committee.
- Add search firm costs to the budget.

Even if you decide to use a professional search firm, the committee still has work to do. For example:

Establish ED Core Competency Requirements

In Part I of the toolkit, we discussed the need for a review of the ED core competencies' document as part of the development of an ED succession plan. Here is where that preliminary work really pays off. If the board has already reviewed and approved the ED core competencies and revised the ED job description, the search committee will not have to redo it.

The ED core competencies must be tied directly to the core elements assessments, like the one in Addendum B. This foundational document provides the basis for the ED job description and performance review. It also becomes the criteria on which the search committee bases their review of potential ED resumes.

I developed this competencies' list based on my own experiences as an ED and CEO in five different nonprofits, ranging in size from a single staff organization to a $6 million nonprofit with 300 staff. It is the rare ED who will come into a nonprofit with all these skills, but these can be the benchmarks or ideals to strive for.

A search committee can use a core competency form like Addendum B either as a rating sheet to score candidates' resumes or send it to candidates to rate themselves. Revise the form to fit the needs of your organization.

The key is to build consistency in all the documents used by the search committee: the ED job description, the rating scale for resumes, and interview questions. This removes the emotions and increases objectivity.

You will be more apt to hire the right ED if the search committee takes the time to solidify these documents first. Remember, the best EDs are generalists, with competencies in all the core elements.

Agree on What the Nonprofit Needs

Before you start interviewing the final candidates, the search committee and board MUST agree on the type of ED you need.

Too many times the hiring process is filled with emotional or political lobbying, rather than fact-based decision making. Whether we like it or not, we often judge people based on the way they look, rather than on their credentials. Sometimes our decisions are based on the fact they are a relative or a colleague. There should never be lobbying by board member, staff or people in the community who try to sway the search committee or executive committee to hire a specific individual for a position. This is often what happens when a much-loved senior staff person applies for the ED position.

The search committee must be as objective as possible, looking for the best person for the position;

someone who can take the organization to the next level and build in long-term sustainability.

Agree on a Timeline

Hiring a new ED takes time. It can easily take up to a year or more but agree on a timeline at the beginning. Consider the following rough timeline:

- Two to three months: Search committee training and preparation
- Two to three months: Advertise the position
- Two to three months: Review resumes
- Two to three months: Interview finalists
- Two months: Selection and orientation of finalist.

Conduct Interviews

Let's assume the search firm or committee have reviewed all the resumes and narrowed it down to the top ten or twelve. They can be interviewed by the search committee via telephone conference call. Sample questions might include:

1. What do you think are the most important duties of an ED?
2. Why do you feel you are the best candidate for the job?
3. What skills do you bring to the job which you think our nonprofit needs right now?
4. What are the most pressing issues facing our community which our nonprofit should be addressing?
5. How do your skills mesh with our vision and mission?
6. Are you a change agent or a maintainer?
7. What would you see as your most important tasks during the first six months on the job?

8. What is the role of the board of directors?
9. Based on the core competencies form, how qualified do you think you are for the job? *(This would be a good question for the final candidates after you have provided them with the core competencies document)*

A form to use for rating the responses is also helpful. For example:
- Response too vague = 2
- Response good = 3
- Excellent response = 5

Check References

Narrow the number of finalists down to three to five. Decide ahead of time when you will check references on the finalists: before or after the interviews. Remember, some employers are hesitant to give any type of detailed references, afraid of lawsuits. Talk to a labor-law attorney or someone familiar with human resources issues to find out the types of questions you can ask when checking references from former employers or leaders within the communities where the finalists worked. References are easy to fake, so check them. Reference questions might include:
- Core competency skills
- Past experiences and behaviors
- One hypothetical question

Don't forget to do criminal background checks at the local, state and federal levels. Unfortunately, there are people who hop from job to job within the nonprofit sector who have been accused of embezzlement. But, they got away with it because their employer was embarrassed and did their best to keep the news quiet. Also check profiles on Facebook, LinkedIn, or other social media sites.

Conclude the Process

Once the search committee recommends a finalist to the executive committee and the hiring decision is made, the board chair should call the candidate and offer them the job. The decision as to whether to get the full board approval for the candidate is up to you. Usually it is better to not do this, since negotiations on salary and benefits occur during this phase of the hiring and you don't want everyone knowing the details. Generally, the executive committee is given the authority to do the hiring of the ED.

After the new ED is hired, notify the board and the personnel department, who will make sure all new-hire information is given to the ED, a starting date is set, and benefits solidified. Some larger nonprofits negotiate contracts, but generally a statement of understanding which outlines the terms of the hiring and benefits is sufficient.

Determine ahead of time who will notify staff and media. The search committee chair should send thank-you notes to committee members and all the candidates who submitted resumes.

Chapter Five: Orientation of the ED

The search committee work is done. The executive committee has selected the finalist, who has accepted the position. Now what?

This is sometimes where the best laid plans fall apart. Without planned orientation, the new ED can be left to flounder around, not knowing the organization, staff, volunteers or the community. There are several things the board chair or executive committee can do to help bring the ED up to speed.

First, decide who will be the most appropriate person to do the orientation. If the former ED is retired, for example, and still in the area, they might be willing to help. Be cautious about this, however, since the former ED will bring their own biases to the orientation.

Usually, the board chair is the most appropriate person to conduct the orientation, unless they are new to their position and don't know much more than the in-coming ED. Another option is to have various members of the executive committee take on various aspects of the training. Possible subjects to cover include:

- Review of the bylaws
- History of the nonprofit
- Overview of the programs
- Review of staff and volunteer organizational charts
- Review of calendars for board, committee and other events
- List of important people to meet and why
- Priority list of tasks to work on from the board

- Review of the strategic plan
- Review of the budget, audit and most recent financial statements
- Review of all policies and procedures

If you ignore the orientation, someone else might step into the vacuum and provide bad information to the new ED.

In one community, a power-hungry real estate broker wined and dined the new ED when no orientation was conducted. He introduced her to local dignitaries and after about a month hinted he would be interested on becoming a board member. Appreciative of his help, she suggested his name to the nominating committee. The day after he was elected to the board, he walked into her office and told her his first goal as a board member was to get her fired. Obviously, he nurtured the new ED and came on to the board for the wrong reasons.

One of the most helpful things I learned to do whenever I came into a new community as the ED was to set up interviews with the board and key leadership in the community. I would either go to lunch with them, or meet at their offices and ask them the following questions, writing down their answers:

- Why is the nonprofit important to the community?
- Why are you involved with the non-profit (or not involved)?
- What do you think should be my priorities during my first year as the ED?
- Who do you think are the five most important individuals I need to meet?

After doing all the interviews, I compiled a great survey of the community, my priorities and a list of key leadership. Plus, I made some great friends and connections within the community.

Chapter Six: Evaluating the Search Process

Once the ED is hired and orientation is completed, it is vitally important for the search committee to do a thorough evaluation of the search process: what worked, what didn't work, what should be done differently next time.

The lessons learned need to be put in writing and the policies and procedures for the next search process revised accordingly.

Unfortunately, the job tenure for EDs in the nonprofit sector is not long, with an average length of stay ranging from two to five years. And, sometimes the length of stay might be because the initial search process was sloppy, resulting in the hiring of the wrong ED.

Some things to evaluate about the search process include:

- Timeline: Was there adequate time allowed for every aspect of the search process? Write down any suggestions for increasing or decreasing time spent on the process.
- Professional search firm: What was the reason for hiring, or not hiring, a professional search firm? Clearly state the reasons to guide the next search committee.
- Interim ED: Why did you decide to hire, or not hire, an interim ED? Again, be clear about the rationale and how it helped or hindered the nonprofit during the transition to the new ED.

- Transition: Was the organization properly prepared for the new ED? What could have been done differently to make the transition easier?
- Budget: Was the amount designated for the search process adequate?
- Search committee: What worked or did not work with the chair, the committee members, and the search process? Be brutally honest so the next search committee doesn't make the same mistakes, if there were any.
- Orientation of ED: How smoothly has the ED transitioned into the position? What other orientation strategies could have been incorporated?

Establishing ED succession plans and the policies and procedures for the search process will take time and effort. But the results will provide long-term benefits for the organization, since hiring the right ED might be the key to long-term sustainability and growth for your nonprofit.

ADDENDUMS

ED Job Description – Addendum A

Title: Executive Director (ED)

Responsible to: The direct supervisor of the ED shall be the chairman of the board, but the ED is responsible to the board for fulfillment of board-approved job objectives.

Key responsibilities: The ED shall be responsible for, or cause to be implemented, all internal and external operations of the nonprofit and the fulfillment of all board approved policies, including:

- <u>General management, relationship building and community involvement</u> – Provides community leadership through collaborations and community problem solving; relationship builder; effective communicator; mature self-confidence; provides ethics and values-driven commitment standards; knows how to facilitate and train volunteers and staff in effective meetings; manages time efficiently and effectively; able to balance work and personal life
- <u>Administration</u> – Responsible for all internal operations; financial and resource management skills, including establishing internal controls; effective staff leadership and understands HR issues; understands facilities and accessibility issues; able to provide accelerating technology leadership; understands risk management and legal issues; knows how to develop work-plans based on on-going strategic planning and comprehensive assessments; knows how and when to outsource
- <u>Board and volunteer management</u> – Responsible for oversight of all volunteer programs; Understands the role of the board and lines of authority between board and staff; understands the differences between

policy and procedures; understands the various board governance structures and how to identify which is appropriate; knows how to recruit, train, recognize and dismiss board, committee and program volunteers; understands committee structures; knows how to promote board involvement in on-going strategic planning; knows how to implement volunteer and staff succession planning; able to lead the board in developing the ED performance review plan

- <u>Program Management</u> – Oversight of the staff or volunteers responsible for the development and implementation of all programs approved by the board; understands and can implement outcomes measurements and can track program effectiveness; able to evaluate program effectiveness; able to juggle differences between donor demands and client needs; understands and incorporates ethnic and demographic challenges

- <u>Marketing</u> – Oversight of staff or volunteers responsible for the development and implementation of a year-round marketing plan, publicity campaigns, and all aspects of building brand identity and positive public relation, including regular assessments

- <u>Resource Development</u> – Oversight of the volunteers or staff involved in all aspects of resource development, fundraising and planned-giving for the nonprofit; able to make fundraising appeals; knows how to evaluate and diversify resource development efforts and develop contingency or reserve funding plans

- <u>Strategic Planning</u> – Upon completion of the board-directed strategic planning process, to implement the strategic plan through staff and volunteer workplans with measurable outcomes and timelines, reporting progress to the board.

Skills Required: Scores high in all the core competencies (Addendum B); ability to work effectively with the board and volunteers; excellent communicator (both verbal and written); working knowledge of resource development, financial management, and program development.

Education Required: Bachelor's degree or master's degree equivalent with emphasis on nonprofit management; minimum of three to five years' experience as ED.

Salary Range: $60,000 to $100,000, depending on experience

ED Core Competencies – Addendum B

Score each area with 1-5. "5" = excellent and "1" = no knowledge in this area. After completing the assessment, total your scores. This assessment is a guide to assist the executive director in identifying areas needing improvement or more education. It is not a scientific or complete assessment but a guide or tool for self-improvement and correlates with Addendum A (ED job description) and the ED performance review. Add or subtract skills required for your nonprofit. This could also be used as part of the search process for finalist candidates.

Core Competency:
General Management, relationship building and community involvement

Score	Skill
	Relationship builder; encourages differing ideas and opinions
	Effective communicator and listener
	Mature self-confidence
	Provides ethics and values-driven commitment standards
	Provides clear direction and sense of priorities
	Makes tough, courageous decisions
	Creates energy and enthusiasm, mobilizing staff and volunteers for action
	Manages time efficiently and effectively
	Able to balance work and personal life
	Provides community leadership through collaborations and community problem solving
	Able to adapt management style to fit the needs of the nonprofit

©2017, Nonprofit Management Simplified, CharityChannel Press

	Effective public speaker
	Total Score (60 possible)

Core Competency: Administration

Score	Skill
	Financial and resource management skills, including the ability to establish internal controls
	Understands budget development and implementation
	Able to convey financial information in an easily-understood format to volunteers, staff and community
	Effective staff leadership by supporting, coaching and encouraging
	Understands facilities and accessibility issues, including ADA (Americans with Disabilities) requirements
	Able to provide accelerating technology leadership
	Understands all risk management issues, such as insurance, disaster preparedness, cybersecurity, abuse and harassment prevention, document storage etc.
	Able to assure nonprofit meets all legal requirements, including federal, state and local tax and/or document filing issues
	Knows how to develop staff work plans based on never-ending strategic planning and comprehensive assessments
	Knows how and when to outsource
	Able to implement long-term sustainability strategies across all facets of the nonprofit

Score	Skill
	Maintains institutional memory through regularly updated policies and procedures manuals
	Creates effective organizational structure
	Able to make tough staffing decisions
	Understands and implements good, legal personnel strategies and policies
	Focuses on staff results and measures staff on outcomes
	Total Score (80 possible)

Core Competency: Board and Volunteer Development

Score	Skill
	Understands the role of the board and lines of authority between board and staff
	Understands the differences between policy and procedures
	Understands the various board governance structures and how to identify which is appropriate for the nonprofit
	Knows how to promote board involvement in on-going strategic planning and acts as a catalyst for needed change
	Knows how to implement volunteer succession planning on the board and committees
	Able to lead the board in developing the ED performance review plan
	Understands committee structures
	Knows how to recruit, train, recognize and dismiss board, committee and program volunteers
	Able to mobilize volunteers to action

	Knows how to deal with ineffective board members
	Understand and handles well the paradox of leading and being led by volunteers
	Knows how to recruit and maintain high-capacity volunteers
	Knows how to set up a volunteer development program
	Total Score (65 possible)

Core Competency: Resource Development

Score	Skill
	Able to make fundraising appeals
	Understands all facets of leadership giving
	Adept at in-kind and planned giving approaches
	Knows how to evaluate and diversify resource development efforts
	Able to develop contingency or reserve funding plans
	Total Score (25 possible)

Core Competency: Marketing

Score	Skill
	Understands and knows how to implement brand identity
	Knows how to develop, implement and evaluate marketing plans
	Knows how to motivate volunteers to promote positive public relations
	Total Score (15 possible)

Core Competency: Programs

Score	Skill
	Knows how to develop an outcomes measurements strategy for all programs
	Able to implement program evaluation strategies
	Able to juggle the differences between donor demands and client needs
	Understands and incorporates ethnic and demographic challenges
	Able to assist program staff in developing strategic goals, work plans for implementation of goals, and budgets
	Able to evaluate programs to ensure they fit with the nonprofit's vision and mission
	Able to make tough decisions when programs are no longer a fit with the vision and mission or are not economically feasible
	Knows how to incorporate volunteers into program efforts legally, without taking staff jobs
	Total Score (40 possible)

Grand Total Possible: 285

285-270 = Excellent
269-255 = Good
254-239 = Needs improvement
238 and below = Poor

ED Succession Planning Committee Job Description
Addendum C

Title: Executive Director Succession Planning Committee/Task Force
Committee/Task Force is the preferred term to avoid confusion with the governing board.
Reports to: A governing board of directors
Selected by: *Committee/Task Force members are appointed by Board Chair to formulate a draft ED Succession Plan for review by Personnel Committee of the Board, review and approval by governing Board.*
Term: The term length of appointed is to create plan or if needed execute ED Succession Plan.
Attendance: *Usually depends upon the tasks assigned to the advisory board. Specific attendance policies should be implemented*
Committee/Task Force Role and Expectations:
1. Demographic representation – Responsible for representing the interests of the nonprofit, entity or individual who appointed the advisory board member
2. Advisory – Does not set policy but recommends actions or policies to the governing board and/or staff
3. Education – Takes the initiative to become knowledgeable about ED succession planning requirements and the nonprofit, programs and policies of the organization
4. Communication – Maintains open communication with staff and other Committee/Task Force board members
5. Support – Provides positive support of the organization to the public

6. Research – Conducts necessary research or study to support input to the board

Expenses: Any expenses associated with the position are generally covered by the appointing entity

Planning Responsibilities and Duties: Play the lead role in working with the executive and key management staff in the develop of succession plans that incorporate the agencies various nonprofit funders relationships, obligations and operations, nonprofit stakeholder groups and possible challenges and scenarios that could arise.

- **Determine your objective and determine if you are planning for** emergency succession planning or formal ED succession planning with more preparation and capacity building time. You can plan for both situations in your plan.

- **Link to nonprofit strategic directions and goals**: The committee/task force members should be familiar (or become familiar) with the nonprofit strategic plan, directions and or/ goals and understand the needed ED abilities and skills requirements. If the nonprofit does not have an updated strategic plan, directions or goals, the committee/task force should recommend to governing board a nonprofit self-assessment and planning process. Time constraints will influence the scope of work for planning process.

- **What are the executive director skills and competencies needed?** Based on nonprofit strategic directions and goals, review of nonprofit growth and current obligations, nonprofit existing management and/or staff development activities or transition preparation, ED annual evaluation, update the ED job description for the future position search.

- **Participants:** Involve board members and key management/senior staff in the input, discuss, and planning process. Build nonprofit-wide ownership in plan, to assure smoother implementation period.

Boards of Directors Job Descriptions
Addendum D

Title: Administrative or Team Board Job Description

Selected by: *Because administrative boards are generally start-up boards, or are involved with organizations with no paid staff, members are usually self-selected initially, but can also be recruited by other start-up or charter board members*

Term: *While a limitation of terms is generally desirable, start-up administrative boards usually do not have terms until the organization hires its first staff. Recommended terms would be three, two-year terms, or two, three-year terms*

Attendance requirements: *Given the lack of staff, administrative boards often meet on a daily or weekly basis. Attendance at such meetings should be mandatory, with resignations accepted after missing two to three meetings in a row*

Responsibilities: *Because there is no staff in the organization, administrative boards function as unpaid staff, the governing board and an advisory board. Responsibilities may include (but are not limited to) the following:*

1. Policy – To consider, approve and support management policies that promote and enhance the mission of the organization
2. Public Relations – To represent the nonprofit to the public, including speaking presentations to potential donors or foundations
3. Fundraising – To plan, execute and evaluate all fundraising efforts
4. Management – To assure development, execution and evaluation of solid infrastructure systems such as: financial management, facilities, program

©2017, Nonprofit Management Simplified, CharityChannel Press

development, marketing, volunteer recruitment, recognition and training, community involvement; strategic, long-range planning and evaluation systems

5. To assist in moving the organization to the point of hiring staff and, once staff is hired, to assist in moving the board to a governing board away from administrative oversight

Commitment:
1. To contribute time, money and resources; to prepare for meetings or administrative tasks by reading background material and soliciting assistance from similar nonprofits or programs

2. To avoid conflicts of interest and, if such a conflict does arise, to declare the conflict to the board and refrain from voting on relevant issues

Expenses: *Since there is no paid staff, administrative expenses of board members are often paid (e.g. postage, copying, purchase of supplies, etc.), although travel, meals and time are usually not paid to the volunteer board*

Time Commitment: *Varies, depending on the number of other board members involved. If acting as a start-up administrative board, it could involve one to two hours per week*

Title: Governing Board Job Description

Selected by: Nominated and selected by members of the governing board

Term: *Generally, three, two-year terms, but not to exceed six years total without the board member taking at least one year off the board*

Attendance: A minimum of 50% of the scheduled meetings per year. Unexcused absence from two consecutive meetings constitutes a resignation

Responsibilities: (as stated in the corporate bylaws) "…The affairs of the Corporation shall be managed by its Board of Directors…"

1. Policy – To consider, approve and support management policies that promote and enhance the mission of the organization
2. Public Relations – To report to and represent the organization in a positive manner to the public
3. Fundraising – To support the organization with personal contributions and to actively participate in the raising of funds to support the organization
4. Advisory – To act as an advisor to the staff by serving on at least one board committee
5. Legal – To exercise fiduciary and legal responsibility for the affairs of the corporation
6. Planning—To develop and monitor short and long-term strategic plans that enhance and support the vision and mission of the organization
7. Executive director oversight – To recruit, train, supervise and terminate the ED
8. Fiduciary – To assure the nonprofit meets the basic Standards of Accounting for Nonprofits and that the financial policies and procedures are followed by staff; to assure the financial stability of the nonprofit

Commitment:

1. To contribute to discussions at meetings, having read background materials and to contribute individual skills and resources as appropriate
2. To observe parliamentary procedures
3. To avoid intruding into administrative issues that are the responsibility of the staff, except to assure their adherence to policy
4. To avoid conflicts of interest and, if such conflict does arise, to declare the conflict to the board and refrain from voting on relevant items

5. To attend governing board meetings, committee meetings, annual meetings and other events which enhance board skills and knowledge

Expenses: Any expenses associated with attendance at events or meetings are the sole responsibility of the board member

Time Commitment: A minimum of 50% of scheduled meetings, plus the annual meeting and other special events or fundraisers. At a minimum, board membership will require two to four hours per month

ED Search Committee Job Descriptions
Addendum E

Title: Executive Director Search Committee Chair
Reports to: Board Chair
Responsibilities:
1. Communications – Keep the board chair informed throughout the process
2. Search Committee selection – To select committee members (No more than seven; no staff)
3. Train committee members – Train members on their duties, using the board-approved job description
4. Facilitation – Conduct meetings and ensure meeting notes are recorded and copies given to board chair
5. Communicate with the executive committee on how the finalists were selected
6. Determine the final terms of the offer for the final candidate with the board chair
7. Develop the orientation strategies for the new ED with the board chair
8. Evaluate the process with the committee after the process, noting what worked and what did not work.

Title: Executive Director Search Committee
Reports to: Search Committee Chair
Responsibilities:
1. Assessment – Develop a system to evaluate the condition of the nonprofit's governance, policies, procedures, strategic plan and board involvement to determine the type of executive director the organization needs
2. Develop the committee job description and send it to the board for approval

3. Develop the budget and timeline for the search process and submit to the board for approval
4. Develop or review the ED job description and core competencies and send to the board of directors for their approval
5. Establish and implement a system for advertising, receiving and rating resumes based on the organizational assessments, job description and core competencies, and selecting candidates for the final three to five candidates for a short-list for interview by the executive committee; develop standard questions for all interviews
6. Ensure reference consent forms are obtained from candidates and professional references and background checks are completed on the finalists
7. If, after executive committee review of the finalists, they are not satisfied, to select additional candidates for their review
8. Contact unsuccessful candidates to thank them for participating in the process
9. Review the search process and make recommendations for future search processes

ED Resume Rating Scale – Addendum F

RATING SCALE

Name: _____

Interviewer:

_____

Position applied for: Executive Director

Date: _____

*Score: "5" = excellent or priority. Score 1-5

Responsibility (based on the core competencies – Addendum B)	Priority level for job*	Score by Interviewer*
Experience as ED (more than 5 years)	5	
Core competency: General Management, relationship building and community involvement	5	
Core competency: Administration - Financial management	5	
Core competency: Administration - Facilities and equipment, technology	5	

©2017, Nonprofit Management Simplified, CharityChannel Press

Core competency: Administration - Risk management	5	
Core competency: Administration - Human resources management	5	
Core competency: Administration - Legal issues	5	
Core competency: Resource development	5	
Core competency: Board & volunteer development	5	
Core competency: Strategic planning	5	
Core competency: Marketing & brand identity	4	
Core competency: Community involvement	4	
Core competency: Programs	4	
Master's degree	4	
Total	66	

About the Authors:

Ron Soto, M.S.W, M.P.H, considers himself blessed to combine his personal mission with his career path for more than 35 years. He brings years of successful executive, management, service delivery, and consulting and training experience with county and city governments, United Way, and small and developing private nonprofits.   His master's degrees are in Social Work and Public Health from the University of California, Berkeley. Other credentials include; Certified Fund-Raising Executive, California State Community College Instructor, Public Service and Administration, California State Community College Counseling, and training in Evidenced-based Youth Services Practice. Ron Soto Consulting, based in San Jose, CA, offers high quality cost-effective management consulting, training and development services to public and private nonprofit agencies.

Connect with the Author
Ron Soto, MSW, MPH
ronsotoconsulting@fastmail.fm
www.ronsotoconsulting.net

Marilyn L. Donnellan, MS, has more than 35 years' experience as a nonprofit CEO and consultant. The nonprofits where she served ranged in size from a single staff organization with a budget of $150,000 to a $6 million nonprofit with 300 staff. She is the author of numerous articles in nonprofit trade journals and her books on nonprofit management are in use in more than a dozen countries. She has a B.A. degree in Human Resources Management from George Fox University and an M.S. degree in Administration from Atlantic Coast Theological Seminary.

Other Books by Donnellan
Available at www.amazon.com/author/mldonnellan :

The Complete Guide to Church Management (English), Xulon Press

Nonprofit Management Simplified: Internal Operations, ©2017, CharityChannel Press

Nonprofit Management Simplified: Board and Volunteer Development, ©2017, CharityChannel Press,

Nonprofit Management Simplified: Programs and Fundraising, ©2017, CharityChannel Press,

Nonprofit Toolkit #1: Volunteer Handbooks

Nonprofit Toolkit #2: The Top Twenty Sustainability Strategies

Nonprofit Toolkit #3: Becoming a Tech-Focused Nonprofit

Two Faces of Me (auto-biography), Halo Press

Give 'til it Hurts (fiction)

Available at www.mldonnellan.com :
Training Modules (companions to the *Nonprofit Management Simplified* books; includes PowerPoint, instructor notes, agenda and sample handouts

Connect with the Author
Marilyn L. Donnellan, MS
mldonnellanauthor@gmail.com
www.mldonnellan.com
www.amazon.com/author/mldonnellan

©2017, Nonprofit Management Simplified, CharityChannel Press

www.ingramcontent.com/pod-product-compliance
Lightning Source LLC
Chambersburg PA
CBHW052339220526
45472CB00001B/495